Rockin' the Class of 1985

The Music That Made Us

Scott Robinson

ISBN 979-8336524864

Cover art by 100 Covers
Author photograph by Joshua Robinson

Happy birthday, Danny!

Also by Scott Robinson ...

The Music that Made Us

Rock Candy: The Beatles

Rock Candy: Elton John

Rock Candy: Def Leppard

Rock Candy: Millennials

Rock Candy: Boston

Rock Candy: Kansas

Rock Candy: Yes

Rock Candy: The Beatles, Vol. II

Born in 1967: The World You Grew Up In

Table of Contents

Introduction

The music of our youth is part of what makes us the grown-ups we become. It's true of every generation: music is ever-changing, but those songs and singers and bands that formed the soundtrack of our teenage years will never leave us.

So it was for those who came of age in the early Eighties – Gen X, we call them now. Full disclosure, though I've written the pages that follow from an inclusive "we", this was in fact the era of one of my brothers; I was a few years ahead. But as all of these songs and bands were surging onto the radio – and the emergent MTV – I was still in my formative phase, and embraced them all.

I hope this retro journey brings back some great memories! It surely has for me.

STR
August 2024

Seventh Grade (1979-80)

Summer break

The summer between the end of elementary school and the beginning of junior high school! A truly transitional corridor of time, connecting two very different worlds, as we stare into the abyss of puberty and realize that all the accumulated social cred we scrambled for as we soldiered through 5th and 6th grade is about to vanish as we mix into the populations of other grade schools into the seething morass of High School Lite!

Well, the Knack had our backs, kicking off our summer with "My Sharona", a mindless headbanger of a song that was as breezy and undemanding as our school's-out mood! Right alongside it was Anita Ward's "Ring My Bell", with its puzzling but enticing euphemism, and the funky "Rise" – a trumpet song? – that we frankly didn't get, but Mom and Dad liked it when it came on in the car.

We remembered Michael Jackson from those cereal box records when we were preschoolers, and now he was back with "Don't Stop 'Til You Get Enough", singing like a grown-up. And "Bad Case of Loving You"? We'd never heard of Robert Palmer, but when that chorus came around – *Doctor, Doctor, gimme the news, I got a – bad case! of lovin' you!"* – we were all over it.

We were likewise singing along – and banging heads – to "Highway to Hell", but only when Mom and Dad weren't in the car. And, in a mellower groove, there was the Little River Band: *Time for a cool change, I know that it's time for a cool change...*, and when the whole band came in on the chorus vocals, we were right there with them.

The ways of love were yet beyond us, but we got an unsolicited lesson from a band called Journey with "Lovin', Touchin', Squeezin'", which seems to take a dim view of relationships in general, flat-out dragging them into adolescent tantrum in the coda. But hey, it's a sing-along, and the Beatles themselves did a *na-na* song, right?

It was a summer for big monster chorus hooks, to be sure, as ELO served up its biggest ever – "Don't Bring Me Down", with its stompy beat and through-the-roof harmonies. *Are they saying 'groose'???*

We had no trouble grasping *Off the Wall* – yup, that's Michael Jackson, and he looks pretty much the same (though that sure as hell wouldn't last) – but we needed to have our older siblings explain who Led Zeppelin was, and why *In Through the Out Door* made them so mopey.

Fall Semester

The endless embarrassments, roiling insecurities and subtle humiliations of life in a much bigger school made Top 40 radio a much-appreciated comfort and solace – a welcome distraction at worst, a reassuring inspiration at best. And good for humorous diversion, when the agonies of the day overwhelmed.

That breathtakingly stupid Piña Colada song by Rupert What's-His-Name was always good for a laugh, and on top of it, we sometimes found ourselves singing along, which somehow made it funnier. Styx's "Babe" didn't go down so easily; wasn't this the band that did "Come Sail Away", the song our older siblings loved so much, the one we always asked our parents to turn up when it came on in the car? Why do they sound like Barry Manilow now?

"Dream Police" brought us back in, giving us a song that wasn't quite an anthem, but we sang it like it was. Lots of that dream stuff going around: *Dreamin' is free,* Blondie assured us.

And as most of us started crushing on some new somebody, causing us to remember with great misery some old somebody, the Commodores let us know they felt our pain with "Still".

Football season! Parents allowing, we'd go to the nearby high school above our middle school as the evenings cooled off, and started hearing an amazing marching band song: "Tusk", which we were astounded to learn was a Fleetwood Mac song.

The romantic agonies to come were further teased by those damn Eagles with "Heartache Tonight", a bold assurance that whatever happened next in our romantic blossoming, it likely wouldn't improve over time. The Police weren't much help: *"Love can mend your life or love can break your heart,"* Sting revealed in "Message in a Bottle". Yeah, thanks for that.

Ah, but then came Queen, and we knew from our "We Will Rock You" days that we could count on them! *"I gotta be cool... relax! Get hip and get on my tracks!"* sang our beloved Freddie, *"There goes my baby, she knows how to rock and roll! She drives me crazy... she leaves me in a cold cold sweat!"* Thank you, Freddie!!! *I kinda like it! Crazy little thing called love...*

Gloria Gaynor then proceeded to kinda rain on it all with her fist-waving "I Will Survive", and then the Captain & Tennille just plain grossed us out with "Do That to Me One More Time".

Enough of this lovey-dovey stuff! Pre-Algebra is hard! So Pink Floyd, which our older sibs had always had on in the basement rec room when they wouldn't let us come down, gives an anthem that speaks our pain:

"We don't need no education! We don't need no thought control! No dark sarcasm in the classroom! Teacher, leave them kids alone!"

And as the holidays approached, we had some new guy, Tom Petty, telling us not to do him like that, and finished the year with a treat: a band named after Dorothy's dog (don't we already have a Kansas?) with a song called "99" that was beautifully strange.

Spring Semester

Back to school after Christmas break – not just a new year, but a new *decade*.

Don't know who Bob Seger is, but this "Fire Lake" is pretty cool. And for the sappy romantics, there was Dan Fogelberg's "Longer" and Air Supply's "Lost in Love". Fleetwood Mac's Stevie Nicks did her witchy thing again with "Sara", and we made a mental note that we really needed to hear more of this Mac stuff. "Sexy Eyes", a little silly, but when big brother/sister pointed out this was the same band that did "The Cover of the *Rolling Stone*", we were more impressed.

"Any Way You Want It" lights up the radio every time it's on, which is a lot, and so we know the name *Journey*. "This is It" was a great song, but we could have done with less of it – the radio played it non-stop. "All Out of Love", Air Supply again – do all their songs have "Love" in the title? "Ride Like the Wind", Christopher Cross, great song! He sounds like a regular guy, like Barry Manilow does, only he's cool. And "I Can't Tell You Why" – that's *the Eagles? Seriously?* Why do they sound like the Bee Gees?

Well, we were still quite young. But we were old enough to know wicked-awesome when we heard it, and Rush's "The Spirit of Radio" was exactly that.

Springtime! The snow melted just in time for Billy Joel, who had abandoned his sport-coat-and-tennis-shoes for a leather jacket, doing some kind of bad-boy rocker vibe with "You May Be Right". Made us wish we were old enough to go out on the weekends.

Ambrosia pushed back on Air Supply with "Biggest Part of Me", only to have Linda Ronstadt wail us back into angst with "Hurt So Bad". Leave it to Paul McCartney to keep us in a good space with "Coming Up".

And as summer beckoned, two new inputs: Bob Seger with the wistful "Against the Wind", with its what-are-we-getting-ourselves-into existential dread: *Wish I didn't know now what I didn't know then...*

And, finally – little Michael Jackson, with the plaintive "She's Out of My Life", which perfectly framed our heartbreak when our crush failed to notice our devotion.

Summer beckoned!

It was a big year at the record store, for those with big enough allowances to afford them. There was the aforementioned *The Wall* by Pink Floyd, the Eagles' *The Long Run*, Mac's *Tusk*, and AC/DC's *Highway to Hell*. There was also a pair of Who albums – *The Kids are Alright* and *Quadrophenia* – and Manilow's *One Voice*, if we were into that sort of thing.

In the Killer Albums from Reliably Awesome Bands bin, there was Foreigner's *Head Games* and *Regatta de Blanc* from The Police. And in the next bin over, I Don't

Know Who This Is But They're Amazing, there was London Calling from The Clash and The B-52s.

Andy Gibb, the baby Gibb, followed in his brothers' footsteps with *After Dark*. A British metal band delivered an album we didn't hear for years – *On Through the Night* – a prelude to our sophomore year of high school, when Def Leppard would take over the world.

But the most amazing musical accomplishment of that first junior high year came from Christopher Cross – the everyguy singer with "Ride Like the Wind". That eponymous album, and its megahit "Sailing", would later sweep up Grammies for Record of the Year, Album of the Year, Song of the Year, and Best New Artist.

We got a big look at Christopher Cross, the B-52s, Pat Benatar – but behind the scenes, a few new bands and artists were in the wings, just out of view: an Indiana boy named Johnny Cougar, a Canadian garage rocker named Bryan Adams. Survivor. The Human League. Orchestral Maneuvers in the Dark. The aforementioned Def Leppard.

We'd hear from them soon enough.

Eighth Grade (1980-81)

Summer break

The first junior high summer is different from all the grade school summers. We're in a bigger world now than we'd been before, and summer is bigger, too: we know more people than we used to; we're learning deeper things; and music has become more important than it used to be.

And into that mix, at the dawn of the new decade, comes Jackson Browne, whom we're not really aware of, with the smooth and sophisticated "Boulevard", the meaning of which is inscrutable to a 13-year old – and Eddie Rabbitt, with "Drivin' My Life Away", which is much easier to decipher but of no lasting relevance.

Elton John introduced us to Little Jeannie as the final seventh grade bell rings, and we have some vague awareness that Elton just keeps changing into someone else all the time, like that alien on *Star Trek*. Grade School Elton sounded nothing like Junior High Elton does.

And Billy Joel? Even worse! "Don't Ask Me Why" is a great song, but wasn't he sneering and party-crashing and being a lunatic just a couple of months ago?

There's this big, bombastic, disco-y anthem from Irene Cara, whom we've never heard of – "Fame", the theme song of a summer movie she's in. It's super-danceable, but of course we don't really know how to dance yet. More accessible is "Xanadu" from Olivia Newton-John, the

Grease Lady – even more danceable, but the movie she's in really blows.

And finally, as summer really starts opening up, two wonderful songs from the Gods of the Sixties, songs that test our growing sense of rock acumen. "Emotional Rescue" from the Rolling Stones puts Mick Jagger into an odd Bee Gees space, which is interesting enough, but what's *really* interesting is that he totally sells it – and it's cool to have that vague sense of comprehension about something working when it oh so shouldn't: but disco, after all, is mostly prancing and preening, and the song is basically Mick's long-overdue *bitch, please!*

But the feel-good song of the summer – and there always has to be one! – is "Let My Love Open the Door", a solo hit from The Who's Pete Townshend. We barely know who The Who are – though that terrible Cincinnati thing was just a few months ago – and the name Pete Townshend isn't yet indelibly inscribed in our craniums. But *what a great song!* We imagine ourselves singing it to our crush...

Fall Semester

Back to school, and we've got this junior high thing down, now: in particular, we are now the upper class, and the incoming seventh graders are the lowly class.

And as we're packing our book bags, there's Queen again. We're still vibing from "Crazy Little Thing Called Love", and here's something even more different – "Another One Bites the Dust", which is ultra-singable and head-bobby and who cares that we have no idea what it means?

Barbra Streisand continues to be better than every other singer around – certainly those summer movie divas – but "Woman in Love" is more a song we imagine our hot English teacher singing along to in the bubble bath. We're all about "Touch and Go", the latest from The Cars, those weird-looking geeks who did "Just What I Needed" and "My Best Friend's Girl", back when we were just kids.

And then suddenly the big song is "Hit Me with Your Best Shot", the hookiest thing we've ever heard from a girl singer who wasn't Karen Carpenter. And then comes the super-likeable "More Than I Can Say", which also sounds like a girl singer, but Leo Sayer is singing own our crushy feelings back at us, so we go with it.

And then, in between Friday night football games, two great new songs landed – songs that sounded *completely different*.

The first was "I Will Follow" – a soaring, exuberant song from a band named – after a spy-plane? U2? And they're *Irish?* That must be it, this tinny, fast rhythm guitar and breathy, overwrought vocal – *Irish* rock, this must be! Okay, it sounds *great*, but what is he talking about?

And Donnie Iris? Skinny Buddy Holly wannabe stepping out of 1958 (except we didn't yet know who Buddy Holly was)? "Ah! Leah!", wow, another great-sounding song, panting lyrics about unspent passions! (Just what our young hearts needed.) But it's the chunky guitar hook and the huge synth break that are really grabbing us: we're hearing the *Eighties*, just around the corner – we just don't know it yet.

When Bruce Springsteen suddenly appears, totally out of the blue, with "Hungry Heart", we might have taken him for somebody new – but no, he's been around for years. Just ask our older brothers! This happy, relatable pop-rocker is simply his very first trip into the Top 10.

And as the leaves have turned, there's Barry Manilow again, who has been living nowhere *but* the Top 10 for most of the past decade. "I Made It Through the Rain" is kind of mopey, but once again, our innocent hearts are teased with the foreshadowing of future anguish.

Less mopey is "Keep on Loving You", a big, wide-eyed ballad from – REO *wut?* Speedwagon? Okay, whatever – great, great song, blissfully insecure, and what a chorus!

And as the leaves fall, another God of Rock surfaces: John Lennon – he was a Beatle, right? - who hasn't been around on our watch at all. His last solo hit, "Whatever Gets You Through the Night", happened when we were all of seven.

But this "(Just Like) Starting Over", wow, what a cool song! It sounds like the Fifties, but it's a song about – well, starting over, and we love it! His buddy Paul, well, he never shuts up, but how great to have another Beatle on the radio!

Except – no. Six weeks later, as the semester is drawing to an end, we hear the terrible news. We've lost him forever.

Christmas break, and we have a buncha great new albums to put on our Christmas lists!

REO Speedwagon's *Hi Infidelity* is up there, and we love Cheap Trick, so *All Shook Up* is good. Those Irish guys have an album called *Boy* that's pretty irresistible – and Springsteen, yeah, he's winning us over, and *The River* seems to be a monster hit.

Our older siblings are lobbying for *One Step Closer*, Doobie Brothers, and *Zenyatta Mondatta* – The Police. And *Gaucho*, Steely Dan. All a little beyond us.

Black Sabbath was before our time, but their singer has gone out on his own. This *Blizzard of Oz* looks promising! Oh, and the B-52s. *Wild Planet*. We'll take it!

And *Double Fantasy*.

Spring Semester

The new year begins with the first flight of the Space Shuttle, so the Alan Parsons Project's "Games People Play" is well-timed; they're kind of spacy. "Rock This Town", Stray Cats, is on the other hand pretty down-to-earth. Dance-in-the-street rockabilly!

Air Supply's "Every Woman in the World" and "Kiss on My List", Hall & Oates, cater to our adolescent longings, as our rock jones is stoked by "Hell's Bells" and "You Better You Bet", from AC/DC and The Who, respectively. Styx throws down some Thinking Rock with "Too Much Time on My Hands", and the Stones are over their disco fit with "Waiting for a Friend". For just plain fun, we have Rick Springfield's "Jessie's Girl", a song for young teenage minds if ever there was one.

Women who sing great are ever more present, and the radio loves "Bette Davis Eyes" and "Angel of the Morning" so much that we're quick to learn the names Kim Carnes and Juice Newton. REO pops up again with "Take It on the Run", a song a little beyond our years, but the ghost of John Lennon lingers with the thoughtful and amiable "Watching the Wheels".

At this point we've well aware that some music is there just to be laughed at, as "Elvira" underscores. Neil Diamond's "America", a goofy patriotic anthem from a really dumb movie of his we saw over Christmas break, is also pretty laughable, but it's hard to beat "Oom-pappa-mow-mow".

"Just the Two of Us" from Grover Washington, Jr. is a mom-and-dad song, but "You Make My Dreams", Hall & Oates, speaks to the pubescent. And this new band – Loverboy? – yeah, "Turn Me Loose" rocks.

So we have Loverboy and a solo Ozzy joining the show. Soon we'll be hearing from some alphabet bands. INXS. R.E.M.

As summer approaches, we're headed to the record store. Styx has a new album out – *Paradise Theater*, their 4th triple-platinum album in a row. Van Halen has another great one, *Fair Warning*, and our big brother asked us to pick up Rush's *Moving Pictures*. And *Face Value* – Phil Collins? Who? From what band? Genesis? What's that?

Freshman Year (1981-82)

Summer break

So long, junior high! You opened up a whole new world for us, transitioning us into the pop/rock landscape with some of the best stuff ever!

A bigger transition still is looming – but as the summer begins, we get another great REO tune – "Don't Let Him Go" – and a new Foreigner track, "Urgent". There's a monster hit from a band our parents like – the Moody Blues – "Gemini Dream". Pretty cool.

And there's a new tune from a new band that jumps right in front of us, "Who Can It Be Now?" from Men at Work – an Australian band? Well, if Ireland can do it, so can they.

As summer rolls open, the divas are out in force, with Juice Newton throwing down "Queen of Hearts" – too clever by half – and "For Your Eyes Only", Sheena Easton, a moody Bond movie song.

The Pointers Sisters? Don't know who they are, really, weren't they very 1972? Well, "Slow Hand" is interesting all the same – a kind of sex talk from your cool aunt, proffering bedroom guidance that teenage masturbation would seem to belie.

"In the Air Tonight" explains that Phil Collins guy, and "We Got the Beat" gives us something new – a girl band, the Go-Go's. And Tom Petty, the guy who told us don't do him like that, now implores us – alongside Stevie Nicks – to stop dragging his heart around.

And, mid-summer – a deceptively unassuming rock ballad that triggers our existential dread: "Who's Crying Now", from a band we've heard before, but are about to hear a *lot* more of: Journey.

The Journey we got from *Escape*, in the record shops in July, alongside the amazing Foreigner *4*; Mac's Stevie Nicks was going it alone on *Bella Donna*, her first solo outing. A new Rolling Stones album – *Tattoo You* - was about to serve up a fantastic back-to-school hit.

And some awfully pretty boys from across the pond dropped a gem named after themselves: *Duran Duran*.

And just before we took the giant leap into high school – we became the class that stepped into young adulthood as music migrated from the radio to cable TV.

We want our MTV!

It was on August 1 that the Buggles' "Video Killed the Radio Star" inaugurated the world's first video cable channel - and we were right there, getting to know Martha Quinn and Mark Goodman and Nina Blackwood and Alan Hunter and JJ Jackson, the original VJs. Killer videos to go with the killer songs we loved! It set off a cultural revolution, launching an unprecedently visual decade of rock – the Eighties.

Fall Semester

So we were rushing home after school to turn on MTV – most of us weren't old enough to have jobs yet – and started getting new tunes not just from the car radio, but from cable TV.

And it was a meaningful respite from a tough day: it's not easy leaving the top rung of junior high for the bottom rung of high school.

MTV and Loverboy eased us through this transition with "Working for the Weekend"... the camera-ready Billy Squier offered up "In the Dark"... the J. Geils Band at their most raucous with "Centerfold"... and the Stones, the classic rock band that was most ideally suited to the video age, with "Start Me Up".

MTV overhauled pop/rock almost overnight. It was no longer how great the song was or how well it was performed; it was now just as important that the video be fantastic.

And Rush's "Tom Sawyer" was. And Olivia Newton-John's "Physical". And "Harden My Heart", from Quarterflash.

Videos, we quickly learned, could be anything. They could be concert footage, which Foreigner loved ("Juke Box Hero", "Waiting for a Girl Like You") – Billy Joel's "She's Got a Way". Stevie Nicks and Don Henley on stage together for "Leather and Lace".

Sometimes the video acted out the song, as Journey did with "Don't Stop Believin'", and Rod Stewart did with "Young Turks". Some were art films, like "Under Pressure" from Queen and David Bowie, which was built on random stock film clips. Some were style pages, like Hall & Oates's "I Can't Go for That (No Can Do)" (quite serious) or "Shake It Up" from The Cars (not so serious).

Then again, some of the new stuff from the Fall of 1981 was distinctly old-school – just well-crafted tunes that made us smile, not particularly MTV-made. Diana Ross's "Why Do Fools Fall in Love. Paul Davis's "Cool Night". "I Wouldn't Have Missed It for the World", from Ronnie Milsap; Dan Fogelberg's "Leader of the Band".

And the Police remained as reliable as ever, finishing out our semester with back-to-back hits – "Every Little Thing She Does Is Magic" in November, "Spirits in the Material World" the following month.

What for Christmas this year? How about *Ghost in the Machine* from the Police, which gave us those great holiday hits? Or Ozzy's sophomore trip, *Diary of a Madman*? Maybe *For Those About to Rock We Salute You*, the latest AC/DC? And you couldn't go wrong with Queen's *Greatest Hits*.

Ozzy wasn't the only lead-singer-gone-rogue; Chicago's Peter Cetera had dropped a solo album.

And there were a couple of mid-schoolyear newbies: Joan Jett? Who loves rock 'n' roll? And a bunch of very leather-bound guys with a funny name? "Mötley Crüe"?

Billy Joel's scraps collection, *Songs from the Attic*, was better suited to our parents, with its late-night lounge feel, and Genesis' *Abacab* was more the terrain of our cool uncles. But *Private Eyes*? We'll take it. And *Shake It Up*, from The Cars? Bring it on, Santa!

Spring Semester

Another new year, and we're halfway through the ritual tortures all freshmen suffer. Joan Jett's jukebox anthem eased our pain, as did some nerdy West Coast throwback named Huey Lewis with the riffy, superfeelgood "Do You Believe in Love", and John Cougar Indiana with his S&M paean "Hurt So Good".

Van Halen's Roy Orbison cover, "Pretty Woman", was goofy as hell, but still made us smile. So did Elton's "Blue Eyes", which set a new record for cornball, but any Elton is good Elton.

Paul McCartney took the feelgood to absurd extremes with "Ebony and Ivory", which even in our freshmen innocence we recognized as dumb schmaltz, Stevie Wonder notwithstanding. We needed some intensity, and Tommy Tutone delivered with "867-5309 (Jenny)", and Asia overdelivered with "Heat of the Moment".

We were through the gauntlet, and ready for summer.

That Asia song came from their debut album, first from a supergroup of ex-Yes, ex-ELP, ex-King Crimson prog rockers (we were too young to know what prog rock was). "Hurts So Good" had come from *American Fool*, and "Pretty Woman" had come from *Diver Down*. *Tug of War* from Paul McCartney was his best solo album since the early Seventies, even if you counted "Ebony and Ivory".

There were also some surprises in the record shop that summer. Iron Maiden, a British band that was overhauling heavy metal from its Black Sabbath origins, delivered *The Number of the Beast*, which was downright literate.

Business as Usual, the first outing of Men at Work, had given us "Down Under". Rick Springfield's *Success Hasn't Spoiled Me Yet* was the rapid follow-up album capitalizing on the previous summer's "Jessie's Girl".

And *Toto IV*, which had given us the breathtaking "Rosanna", was about to go on to sweep the Grammies, racking up Album of the Year, Record of the Year, and Producer of the Year.

Phil Collins and Peter Cetera were old-school veterans stretching their solo artist wings, but there were plenty of genuine freshman out there – Duran Duran, the Go-Go's, Mötley Crüe, and Quarterflash – and also a few we'd soon hear from.

The Thompson Twins.

Wham!

And Tears for Fears...

Sophomore Year (1982-83)

Summer break

No longer the school underclass, we felt our horizons broadening as we rolled into our mid-teens, many of us now firmly focused on the prospect of romantic partners – and adjusting our musical preferences to both inform these impulses and better understand those enticing others who had our attention.

The radio obliged, serving up tunes both inspirational and lascivious as summer commenced: "Dancing in the Street". "Come on Eileen". "Hungry Like the Wolf".

But, reliably, that AM dial provided us balance, with the cautionary "Love's Been a Little Bit Hard on Me" from Juice Newton, and Chicago's penitent "Hard to Say I'm Sorry".

Men at Work resurfaced with its saxy "Who Can It Be Now?"; Steve Miller was new to us (though not at all new to our older siblings), but not for long, offering up his very last #1 hit with "Abracadabra". "Eye of the Tiger" was a movie theme (for *Rocky III*), but we didn't hold that against it; it just cemented our love of Survivor.

And 18 months after that tragic December night when the world lost John Lennon, Elton John offered up a loving tribute – "Empty Garden (Hey Hey Johnny)".

And all of that happened before June!

Kenny Rogers did another mom-and-dad song ("Love Will Turn You Around") and Laura Branigan once again proved herself as powerful and evocative as any pop diva out there with "Gloria".

But it was "Africa" that really made our summer.

Toto's fourth album would be a Grammy juggernaut and a radio bonanza with six singles, three of them Top 10.

"Africa" was a #1. With its veldted rhythms, celestial synthesizers and soaring harmonies, it was a song like nothing we'd ever heard. The MTV video was a little klunky, but it revealed something we'd seldom ever seen: a band with *two* keyboard players. And wow, those two were all over the place!

This was a song we never got over.

Joe Cocker's unlikely teaming with Jennifer Warnes, "Up Where We Belong" was another movie theme – from Richard Gere's *An Officer and a Gentleman* – and was serviceable enough, a feelgood song; but it was "Jack and Diane", from John Cougar Soon-to-be-Mellencamp that was the true feelgood song of the summer.

Simultaneously surging with innocence and hormones, "Jack and Diane" was a couples song all about the endless possibilities of – well, *us*. Kids in their mid-teens. If we were lucky enough to live near a Tastee Freeze, we could drop right into it. Who doesn't love chili dogs? *Hold onto 16 as long as you can...*

That sentiment was self-justifying enough, but this tune also pulled the Midwestern farmboy rocker above his peers, into Woody Guthrie territory, with that almost thrown-away line that told us who he was, and warned us what was in store for Jack and Diane:

Oh yeah, life goes on, long after the thrill of livin' is gone...

Many of us had part-time jobs now. What were we buying in the record store?

Duran Duran's *Rio*, for one, its follow-up to their debut album from the previous year. *Mirage*, from Fleetwood Mac. And both our parents and older siblings could get into CSN's *Daylight Again*.

Fall Semester

Sophomore year! Our back-to-school songs started off with "Rio", and it must be said that Duran Duran was made for MTV! Or maybe the other way around. Either way, rock had never seen boys prettier or more camera-loving than these. Although Stevie Nicks, taking the lead vocal of Fleetwood Mac's "Gypsy", is pretty camera-ready herself. The Clash's "Should I Stay or Should I Go?" was pretty out-of-character, but still a great tune. And Prince owned us with "1999", our dance track of the year.

That fall, pop/rock was all over the place, from the goofy "Dr. Heckyll and Mr. Jive" from Men at Work (yes, we still love you) and Neil Diamond's sappy "Heartlight", to Don Henley's bitchy "Dirty Laundry" and Billy Idol's sneering "White Wedding".

Crosby, Stills & Nash put out "Southern Cross" and it's instantly clear to us why our parents love so much. "Pressure" and "Maneater" (Billy Joel and Hall & Oates respectively) are incredibly uncomfortable, but Supertramp's last hurrah "It's Raining Again" paradoxically cheers us right back up. And the UK one-hit wonder Naked Eyes gives us a huge hook fix with "Always Something There to Remind Me".

Phil Collins finishes out the year for us with a golden oldie – a cover of "You Can't Hurry Love", a Supremes hit from the mom-and-dad years.

What for Christmas? The very introspective among us might have picked up Springsteen's "Nebraska", a masterful collection of songs he recorded alone in his basement – a style of music that would come to be known as 'Americana'.

Michael Jackson changed his hair! What's this *Thriller* thing? And what's this? His baby sister Janet went and made an album? How cute!

"Twisted Sister"? How perfect is that?

Prince's "1999" was a title track, and the album is a monster.

"Night Ranger"? *Dawn Patrol*? Sure, why not?

And finally, if we happened to be in the record store with our older brothers, there was a new album they'd have pounced on - *Three Lock Box*. Why? Because they wore *Montrose* out, back when they were in junior high. And *Three Lock Box* is an album by Montrose's lead singer.

A guy named Sammy Hagar.

Spring Semester

The second half of high school's second year got off to an astounding start, with Journey's warp drive-powered "Separate Ways" (though the video was too stupid to watch all the way through) and a killer track from a new British band with an utterly 1967 name – Def Leppard??? "Photograph" rocked our asses off!

And Michael Jackson? Not cute anymore. "Billie Jean" was as dark and intense as anything we'd ever heard on the radio.

"Sweet Dreams (are Made of This)" – Eurythmics, from England? – very synthy, and likewise pretty intense. And

U2 – we've gotten used to that name now – "New Year's Day"? A political song?

And that's just January.

Michael had blown our doors off with "Billie Jean", then turned right around and rocked us with "Beat It" only a month later. That scorching guitar? Eddie Van Halen.

Bonnie Tyler brought us back to earth with the tortured "Total Eclipse of the Heart", and speaking of hearts, that Canadian kid Bryan Adams comes at us straight from his. Prince follows up "1999" with "Little Red Corvette", and Styx veers wildly off course into Broadway with "Mr. Roboto", which sounds a lot like the Eurythmics, but it's such a great track for dances in the gym that we forgive them.

Irene Cara, the "Fame" singer, gives us an even better dance track with "Flashdance... What a Feeling", and David Bowie (of all people) outdoes them all with "Let's Dance".

Yup, it seems like it's a springtime for dancing. Someday we'll say "Hold my beer", and that's what Eddy Grant would have said when he outdid all of the above with "Electric Avenue".

Men at Work goes from silly to chill with the very cool "Overkill", and U2 gets even more political, if that's possible, with "Sunday Bloody Sunday".

R.E.M.? Who is that? "Radio Free Europe"? and ZZ Top, we know who they are – "Gimme All Your Lovin'"! Power rock for rednecks! We'll take it!

Elton throws down with his self-justifying "I'm Still Standing", and Journey out-power ballads themselves with "Faithfully", to which our crushes swooned.

And as summer beckons, our school year winds down with Donna Summer's working-class anthem "She Works Hard for the Money" and a sacrilegious rape of Irving Berlin's "Puttin' on the Ritz" by some overdressed mannequin named Taco. The Police swoop in to save it, as they always do, with their triumphant stalker hymn, "Every Breath You Take".

Junior Year (1983-84)

Summer break

By the summer of '83, the Eighties had well and truly arrived.

Every new decade takes a few years to establish its own identity, to let the previous one fritter away. The Sixties had persisted until 1972 or so, when our parents reconciled themselves to the end of hippie culture and fully accepted that no, the Beatles weren't coming back. And it was the same for us; by 1983, music had changed completely, now heavy with synthesizers, power chords, and hair gel. The days of blue jeans, facial hair and tie-dye rock were gone.

We had MTV to thank for that, of course, but we were happy to take ownership. We, too, had well and truly arrived; we were full-fledged upperclasspeople, and when we got back to school, we would walk around like we owned the place. Which, of course, we would.

Many of our hearts had broken by now. Much virginity had been lost. And the summer gave us plenty of comfort; Stevie Ray Vaughn's "Pride and Joy" was a truly smile-along, Def Leppard had us banging our heads to "Rock of Ages", and those Men at Work guys had come up with another winner with the apocalyptic "It's a Mistake".

ZZ Top had managed to make Texas raunch sexy with "Sharp Dressed Man", as misogynist a song as we would ever likely hear; Talking Heads flattered our growing self-awareness with the intense "Burning Down the House";

and The Police once again mocked our inadequacies with the deliciously brainy "Wrapped Around Your Finger".

It fell to Billy Joel and Huey Lewis to get our heads in back-to-school mood, with the former did with "Tell Her About It", a celebration of boy/girl synergy that made us feel better about our upcoming prospects; and "Heart and Soul", a feel-good, power-chord riff hook fest that delivered the summer's best video – well, it was that perfect summertime song we had now come to expect.

We dropped lots of our summer-job dollars at the record store, as always, picking up *Pyromania* and *Frontiers* and *Eliminator* – Leppard, Journey, and ZZ – and *Synchronicity* wasn't even a question. The poppier among us grabbed the *Flashdance* soundtrack and Wham!'s *Fantastic*; *Cargo*, from Men at Work, was an easy pic.

Kilroy Was Here, the death knell of our beloved Styx, not so easy. Rock opera from The Who was one thing; from the band that went from "Blue Collar Man" to "Babe"? Not so much. We were more open to U2's *War* and *Speaking in Tongues* from Talking Heads.

And there were a couple of albums from new faces, which many of us checked out: Madonna, from whom we'd hear much, and Weird Al Yankovic – an acquired taste if ever there was one...

Fall Semester

Sure enough, we owned the place. As juniors, we were firmly ensconced in our by-now-well-cultivated bravado/insecurity, well on our way to our next romantic crash-and-burn and social overreach. We had our bouffant hair; we had our Walkmans; we had our MTV!

The Eighties were, after all, the systematic rejection of the Seventies – which we went all in on, turning the station when "Islands in the Stream" came on and cranking the volume for "Love is a Battlefield" and "Union of the Snake". On the other hand, a little nostalgia here and there couldn't hurt, so we gave Billy Joel's "Uptown Girl" a chance. And loved the video with his then-new wife, Christie Brinkley.

Cyndi Lauper justified both our carefree flight and our questionable fashion sense with "Girls Just Wanna Have Fun", which became an anthem, and Culture Club's "Karma Chameleon" reassured us that our embarrassing romantic errors were more feature than bug.

The Police reliably made us feel smart with "King of Pain", as John Cougar Mellencamp reliably made us feel self-conscious with "Pink Houses". Mötley Crüe? Shouting at the devil, their studded leather not clashing at all with their mascara.

Beatle Paul's collaboration with Michael J, "Say Say Say", wasn't anywhere near as embarrassing as "Ebony and Ivory" had been, but as the holidays approached, it was the out-of-the-blue surprises that delighted us: "Owner of a Lonely Heart", a wildly careening sonic dance rocker from... Yes? Seriously? Those hippie dippie proggers who planted their flag in 1971? And Night Ranger – America's Def Leppard wannabes – knocking us out with "(You Can Still) Rock in America".

Elton's slow-down ballad, "Guess That's Why They Call It the Blues" reminded us where we'd come from, but it was those California boys with the clown out front and the wildest guitar since Hendrix that closed out the year like no year had ever been closed out before with – of all things! – a keyboard anthem:

"Jump"...

What's under the Christmas tree? *Sports*, from Huey Lewis and his New; Night Ranger's *Midnight Madness*; Ozzy's *Bark at the Moon*. Yes had knocked us out with "Owner"; their *90125* went to #1, assuring us there was plenty more where that came from. *Colour by Numbers* from Culture Club felt seasonally apropos, as did Lionel Ritchie's *Can't Slow Down*.

But Billy Joel's Fifties callback *An Innocent Man* might have been more a Boomer record, as was Johnny Cash's *Johnny 99* – although the latter channeled Springsteen, which was about as current as you could get.

We'd seen plenty of new bands – Night Ranger, Queensrÿche, Twisted Sister, Ratt, Poison, Europe, Bon Jovi. A Flock of Seagulls. Huey Lewis & The News. And there were lots of new girls on the block, Janet Jackson in particular.

It was the guys who had fronted bands and were now out on their own that seemed to dominate, however. Phil Collins. Lionel Ritchie. Don Henley.

We were definitely gonna see a lot more of that…

Spring Semester

It had been easier for our older siblings – and certainly our parents – to parse musical preference by gender. Everybody loved the Beatles and the Beach Boys, but Black Sabbath and Led Zeppelin tended to be for boys, while girls went for Loggins & Messina, Seals & Crofts, and so on.

That line really blurred with the Eagles and Fleetwood Mac, and in the Eighties it was almost gone: both genders could love Leppard and the Crüe and Night Ranger. The androgyny of Duran Duran and their peers – and, for that matter, every heavy metal band that wasn't Metallica – was palpable.

Still, as 1984 swung open, the ladies had their "Careless Whisper" and "Time After Time" and Julio Iglesias, and the guys could claim "Rock You Like a Hurricane" and "Hot for Teacher".

The genders could agree on "Runaway" and "Sister Christian", and guys could harbor secret affection for "Footloose" while dismissing "Let's Hear It for the Boy".

And "West End Girls", the Pet Shop Boys? Like Tears for Fears, we didn't really know that was. Less masculine, certainly, that Duran Duran et al, but that wasn't saying much; masculinity had all but fled Britain, that nation having no Bruce Springsteen to call its own.

Even so, the year was off to a fresh, eclectic start.

You could see it in the record store, as Van Halen reinvented itself with 1984, as veteran Tina Turner reaffirmed her dominion with Private Dancer. Newcomers Bon Jovi and Ratt delivered strong opening salvos, and Bananarama and Metallica produced respectable sophomore offerings.

But the long-timers truly soared. Queen's The Works. Springsteen's Born in the USA. Prince's Purple Rain. The old guys still had it.

As for faces we hadn't seen yet, but would soon: our junior-to-senior transition ran parallel to the launch of the Black Crowes; Katy Perry; Soundgarden. Living Colour, and the New Kids on the Block. And more British bands with goofy, Sixties names: Big Audio Dynamite. Fine Young Cannibals. The Cult.

Senior Year (1984-85)

Summer break

The final year of high school was just up ahead when the first single from Bruce Springsteen's triumph *Born in the USA* hit the radio. "Dancing in the Dark" was the first in a staggering series of seven single that would spill out of that album, and had an energy and spirit that won over a whole new following for the Boss.

But that wasn't the song of the summer.

Neither was Lee Greenwood's "God the Bless the USA", which was a song for our grandpas, and neither was Tina Turner's "What's Love Got to Do with It" or Prince's "When Doves Cry" – not songs that got us happy and excited.

No guy in the world would get anywhere near "Wake Me Up Before you Go-Go", and few of the ladies would champion Van Halen's "Panama". And the faux rebellion of Twisted Sister's "We're Not Gonna Take It" wasn't in any way inspiring. Or interesting.

How about The Cars? They served up both "Magic" and "Drive" that summer – and the latter was a ballad, not a summer anthem (though it was a great song for parking).

No, it was "Oh Sherrie", from a slumming Steve Perry, taking a break from Journey after back-to-back platinum albums. As hook-ridden and sing-along as anything Journey itself had ever done, this track played endlessly, and was more-or-less gender-neutral – a whiny, driving love song with great guitar riffs.

And now – our senior year!

Fall Semester

The gods of radio were looking after us as we ascended to high school's pinnacle. Stevie Wonder kicked off back-to-school with "I Just Called to Say I Love You", as good-feeling a feel-good song as we could hope for, which Prince followed up with the moody "Purple Rain". Then Queen gave us another monster track, "Hammer to Fall", alongside the Boss's ironic Vietnam elegy, "Born in the USA".

Then we got "Like a Virgin", which lifted Madonna into the heavens, and "Run to You" from Bryan Adams, the first hit single from his first hit album. Tina Turner threw down yet another breathtaking tune, "Private Dancer", and then – out of nowhere – another hair-gel juggernaut from across the Atlantic, Norwegian synth rockers a-ha, took over MTV and our stereos with "Take on Me".

That's a churning, seething mass of eclecticism already, but it got better still as the holidays approached. Foreigner, for years such a reliable source of hedonistic indulgence and emotional distance, offered up "I Want to Know What Love Is", an absolutely celestial paean to ardent devotion. And right next to it, "Shout" – from Tears for Fears – an anthem for all our teenage angst.

And after all the pep rallies and football games and Saturday nights, REO Speedwagon – the "Keep on Loving You" guys from our junior high years – come back with "Can't Fight This Feeling", yet another validation of all our sappy romantic pining.

What for Christmas? Lots to ask Santa for, great new albums landing since the summer. Bryan Adams' *Reckless* was a hit machine, and so was Like a Virgin. Serious old-school rockers could lobby for Foreigner's *Agent Provocateur*, and the brainy ones could hold out for U2's *The Unforgettable Fire* and the Talking Heads' *Stop Making Sense*.

Longtime fans of Barry Manilow were in for a surprise: done with the Top 40, Manilow had rejiggered some old Johnny Mercer songs – stuff our grandparents loved – and gotten a bunch of jazz musicians into a studio to record them. The tape rolled, and they played the first one perfectly. Manilow signaled for everyone to keep going – and they recorded all 10 songs without a single mistake, making 2:00 *AM: Paradise Café* the first (and only) album to ever be recorded in one take.

Don Henley gave us a treat with his solo album *Building the Perfect Beast*, the most not-Eagles album imaginable; Survivor put up *Vital Signs*, its most hit-rich album yet. Wham!'s *Make It Big* was an obvious choice, and for those who wanted something new, there was *The Red Hot Chili Peppers*, from the Red Hot Chili Peppers.

Spring Semester

Our final semester of high school, as it turned out, was more poppy than rock-y: Phil Collins had long since signaled his boredom with progressive rock and seemed determined to pop us silly, which he did once again with "Sussudio". Madonna for sure had our attention now, and

"Material Girl" became an Eighties Grrl anthem that not even Cyndi Lauper could compete with.

A mass collaboration chorused up for "We Are the World", a fundraiser produced by Michael Omartian (the guy who lifted Christopher Cross into the heavens) and Michael Jackson's mentor Quincy Jones. That collaboration included Lionel Ritchie, Stevie Wonder, Bette Midler, Steve Perry, Huey Lewis, Billy Joel, Diana Ross, Bob Dylan, Kim Carnes, Tina Turner, Kenny Rogers, Paul Simon, and a couple dozen other pop/rock giants.

Paul Young gave us a remake of Hall & Oates' "Everytime You Go Away", and Tears for Fears topped themselves with the likeable, sophisticated "Everybody Wants to Rule the World". Duran Duran surprised us with a Bond theme, of all things – the excellent "A View to a Kill".

And now we're done, being fitted for caps and gowns, ready to do our diploma walk. We got the most joyous, celebratory send-off any graduating class could hope for: "And We Danced", from the awkwardly named Hooters, and the Boss's jubilant "Glory Days".

College-bound

One last carefree summer before college! Diplomas in our hands, mortar boards tossed aside – and Bryan Adams paints us with nostalgia that's still fresh from the oven with "Summer of '69", more a Boomer tune than ours (but we still love it!). Dire Straits nods to our ownership of MTV with "Money for Nothing"; Starship, which had once been our parents' Jefferson Airplane, reminded us how silly we looked with "We Build This City".

Then our own USA put up a hair-gel band to rival Britain's best with Mr. Mister, who would rule MTV and the airwaves for the next year, starting with "Broken Wings". Tina Turner delivered yet again with "We Don't Need Another Hero", a movie track (from *Max Mad Beyond Thunderdome*); Loverboy stayed on our radar with "Lovin' Every Minute of It".

Our perfect summertime song came from Huey Lewis & The News – a summertime band if ever there was one – teasing the upcoming megahit Back to the Future with its signature track, "The Power of Love".

And finally, our bags all packed for college, a reinvented Heart leaves "Barracuda" and "Crazy on You" behind with their complete pop make-over "Never" – followed by "Saving All My Love for You", from a new face destined to stand alongside Tina Turner, Gladys Knight, Diana Ross, and Dionne Warwick: Whitney Houston.

One last trip to the hometown vinyl store before college, where we can pick up Whitney's debut album, Dire Straits' *Brothers in Arms*, *Songs from the Big Chair* from Tears for Fears, and Mr. Mister's *Welcome to the Real World*. Heart's new sound oozes from their simply-titled *Heart*; Phil Collins continues his pop crusade with *No Jacket Required*.

David Lee Roth's abandonment of Van Halen has been big news, and he gives us a taste of what comes next with *Crazy from the Heat* – though that's the *least* of what's to come with those guys. John Fogerty, the voice of mom and dad's Creedence Clearwater Revival, is in the bins with *Centerfield* – and we have debut albums from a-ha (*Hunting High and Low*) and the supergroup Power Station.

There's Night Ranger's *7 Wishes*, which is pretty good (and will turn out to be their peak); *Gravity*, from Kenny G; and *Boy in the Box* from Canadian Corey Hart.

The real treasures we're taking off to college with us, however, are *Hold Me* from Laura Branigan, with its moving and melancholy "Forever Young", and J.C. Mellencamp's *Scarecrow*, his best yet, with its Americana anthem "R.O.C.K. in the U.S.A."

And we're off!

Whitney and Power Station are the new faces in our faces, but a few more have set sail and will present themselves very soon: Simply Red; Indigo Girls; Jane's Addiction; Goo Goo Dolls; Crowded House. Extreme. Tesla. And a couple will be *huge*: Bruno Mars. Guns 'n' Roses.

And as we step on campus, we can look back across our teenage years and realize, we had it pretty good. Pretty great!

About the Author

Scott Robinson is a journalist, social scientist, public speaker and musician, and was for 20 years a music critic with the *Louisville Courier-Journal*. He is also a member of the Scottish Society of Louisville. He has also been published in *Rolling Stone* and *The Wall Street Journal*.

He can be reached at

scott.robinson@glenmillscience.com